The Home You Imagine

BE INSPIRED BY THE STORIES OF PEOPLE WHO
ORGANIZED THEIR OWN BEAUTIFUL AND
COMFORTABLE LIVING SPACES

Anita Marie

Discover HERE!

The Home You Imagine

REDUCE & STREAMLINE

Cleaning & Decluttering

Time by 100%

Without The Overwhelm and Make Your Home Stunning!

As a way of saying "thank you" for your purchase, I'm going to share with you a Free Gift that is exclusive to readers of "The Home You Imagine."

Success is YOURS when you use These Time-Tested Tools!

GO HERE TO ORDER - https://bit.ly/TheHomeYouImagineGift

Table of Contents

Introduction: The Power of a Beautiful and Organized Home 1

Chapter One: The Benefits of Decluttering and Cleaning........................... 7

The Benefits... 7

Chapter Two: Getting Started: Preparing Your Mind and Space.................. 12

The Preparation 13

Chapter Three: Decluttering Techniques: Letting Go of Unnecessary Items . 19

The Art of Letting Go... 20

A Clutter-Free Environment... 23

Chapter Four: Cleaning Techniques: Creating a Clean and Healthy Home.. 27

Exploring Effective and Efficient Cleaning Techniques 28

Chapter Five: Designing Your Dream Home: Creating a Beautiful and Cozy
Space.. 38

Vision to Reality.. 38

Chapter Six: Keeping the Momentum Going: Creating Lasting Habits 46

Healthy Routine of Decluttering 47

Chapter Seven: Dealing with Challenges: Overcoming Obstacles 50

Overcoming Obstacles... 50

Chapter Eight: Creating Memories: Living Happily in Your Dream Home.. 58

Happily Ever After 58

Conclusion.. 65

Introduction: The Power of a Beautiful and Organized Home

All's well that ends well.

When you hear this phrase, what comes to mind?

You might recall Shakespeare's comedy about the beautiful woman Helena and her comedic pursuit of a man of a higher social position than her in a French court. At the end of this celebrated play, the character says that the success of an undertaking depends on how everything turns out.

In academic terms, "All's well that ends well" means everything turned out satisfactorily, although the result seemed uncertain at first. Many endeavors start this way, including designing or organizing one's home.

A young mom felt uncertain as she entered the home of her husband's childhood. Don't get me wrong! It's not this old, haunted manor you read about in books. It's just that there's too much stuff!

When her husband's mother passed, she left the house for her son. It was a welcome gift for the family with three children and ever-increasing expenses. They can save the rent money for the kids' future.

But alas! The sizable house was left with a lot of clutter. As his mom aged it was difficult to toss things and the clutter began to accumulate. Everything from her husband's entire childhood was still in the basement. Living there for a while was going to be a blessing for a few years until they could go and buy their own first home. They had to take on this challenge and make it work.

Looking at the situation, the mom felt overwhelmed. How can she do all this? Move their things in and declutter his mom's lifetime collection of belongings simultaneously. They dove in to make it happen by using a system and agreeing on what to keep and what to toss out. At least that was the plan.

The mother called me a few months after they moved in. According to her, the family decided to buy a new home sooner rather than deal with this old house, its issue, and the five-year plan they thought they were going to follow – they wanted their dream home now.

The next step was to visit them at their mom's house. I anticipated seeing a super clean organized house. To my disappointment, it was like walking into a place where a family had just moved in. Essentially, they hadn't made a dent!

The family truly needed help. They were very overwhelmed! This mountain was seemingly too high to climb. It looked like they didn't know how to prioritize tossing things out. Most of the mothers' things were still in the house and now were mixed up with their boxes and their items. What were they to do? They were exhausted and needed my help.

I was excited to help them, everything was solvable. We started with me giving them my success cleaning tips list, an immediate start priority plan as well as suggesting they hire a professional to help them declutter, toss things out yesterday and incorporate the sentimental items they were keeping with their things.

I knew they needed to experience satisfaction and progress sooner rather than later. They bought into my suggestions, and they started to get to work.

With professional help, and improved priorities within four weeks, the house turned into a stunning, organized, decorated masterpiece! So perfect that the family decided to stay. For a little while, at least. WOW ok! I was happy for them. I guess I wasn't putting this baby on the market. It was ready though for whenever that day was to happen. What a change!

Three years later, I got the same call and was told that it was for real this time. They want to sell the house.

"Could you be our realtor?" They asked.

Although I was shocked, I was delighted for the opportunity. They told me that the house remains in perfect condition. Thanks to the idea of prioritizing decluttering and cleaning.

Indeed, the house still looked terrific.

The family is on a roll. They have everything under control now, and they are a far cry from the family I met months before who did not have a clue about what to do with the house.

They had even started packing. They even used all my "getting started" suggestions as the house needed a small bit of tidying up to get it ready to sell.

Here's what they had going on. They wanted to discard even more things in anticipation of moving into a brand-new home. Good for them. They placed five sizable black garden bags strategically around the house.

The children were enlisted to participate in the activity. They were instructed to examine items and discard anything that appeared worthless or rubbish by placing it into one of the black bags. The children thoroughly enjoyed the task.

Everyone experienced a sense of control over the situation. After acquiring 20 plastic containers and a few cardboard boxes, they labeled three of the bins as "permanent belongings," another three as "necessities," and the remaining three as "undecided." You cannot get more organized than this!

They even arranged for certain groups to collect numerous pieces of old furniture, sold a few items on Craigslist, and gave away several other items for free. Additionally, they informed some relatives to take anything they wanted.

They told me their activity even became weekend gatherings with friends and relatives. They took the task of sorting through their belongings seriously and found it enjoyable.

Over a span of one to two weeks, they continued to refine the process, resulting in an immaculately clean house ready for the market. In preparation for selling the property, they even performed minor staging to enhance its appearance.

They enlisted the services of a landscaper who charged them $500 to clean up the garden, spread bark, and plant three attractive trees in the front yard and a stunning huge pot of flowers at the front door. Just the way I like it!

It indeed was an "All's well that ends well" situation.

In case you are wondering, we sold the house right away. At the open house, people said they were shocked at how clean and organized it was.

And what about their new home?

It was immaculate!

Their new home looked fantastic, adorned with some of his mother's beautiful silver items and paintings tastefully placed throughout. They now have a clean and stylishly decorated home that they take pride in.

Having visited their home several times over the years, I can attest to the ongoing success story of an inspiring family who prioritizes living in a tidy and organized environment, frequently decluttering and decorating their home to reflect their personal style.

It's everyone's dream to have a beautiful and organized home. Your home is your haven. No matter how busy you are, you return to your house at the end of each day. Who wants to go home to a messy and disorganized place.

The easiest way to unwind and relax after a rigorous day is at home. And there's no denying that one feels much better if the home you return to is pleasing to the eye.

Also, too much clutter can distract you from things that matter in your life. That's why it is very important to create an uncluttered home.

According to top designers, altering your surroundings can significantly impact your life. Although using top-notch materials, stylish furniture, and appealing embellishments can enhance your living space, eliminating unneeded mess to accommodate the things you genuinely cherish can often create the most significant transformation and improve your home and emotional state.

Getting rid of unnecessary clutter and the emotional weight it carries can be liberating. After spending a morning decluttering, you may feel reinvigorated and motivated to continue cleaning and organizing throughout the day. You can even give the newly cleared spaces a good scrub. The key is to find the drive to begin the decluttering process.

Are you seeking ways to create a clean, cozy, and stylish home without feeling overwhelmed by schedules, checklists, and procrastination? Do you often feel overwhelmed and need help starting home improvement projects? Have you resigned to the idea that your home will always be cluttered and messy?

If you answered yes to all of these questions, then this book is for you. It provides insights and tips to help you create a beautiful, organized home that promotes happiness and success.

Keep on reading. You will soon discover your dream home is buried beneath all that clutter.

Turn your fantasy home into reality!

Chapter One: The Benefits of Decluttering and Cleaning

In our modern society, where material possessions often define our lives, decluttering has emerged as a powerful practice that brings many benefits. Decluttering involves systematically organizing and removing unnecessary items from our living spaces, creating a sense of order and simplicity. Beyond the physical act of tidying up, decluttering can positively impact our mental and emotional well-being.

Let's explore the numerous advantages of decluttering, from reducing stress and increasing productivity to fostering creativity and promoting a more harmonious living environment. By shedding excess belongings and finding solace in a simplified existence, individuals can unlock a path toward a more fulfilling and balanced life.

The Benefits

Creating your dream home is a challenging task. There may be times when you get overwhelmed to the point of giving up.

But don't. Always think of the benefits. Here are some of them.

1. Reduces stress and anxiety

Having a cluttered house can have adverse effects on your mental well-being. It can overwhelm your brain with too much sensory information, leading to feelings of irritability, increased stress levels, and even shame or embarrassment when guests visit.

Additionally, not finding things among all the piles of possessions can be stressful. Your home should be a place of comfort. After a grueling day at work, who would want to face clutter issues at home?

It's time to kick your heels and relax. It's time to have a glass of wine and be calm. A clean and cluttered home will clear your mind and settle your nerves.

2. Encourages creativity and productivity.

One's productivity and creativity can be challenging for many individuals surrounded by clutter. For instance, working at a disorganized and messy desk can hinder concentration as the excess items around you can compete for your attention, leading to decreased output.

By eliminating clutter, your ability to focus should improve, leading to an increase in concentration levels. When you have improved focus and a clear mind, you are more likely to experience a surge in creativity since you can concentrate on the task without being distracted by surrounding objects.

3. Makes you sleep better.

Even if you close your eyes, you are still aware of the mess around you, such as clothes lying on the floor and makeup products scattered on the dresser. Having these things in sight before going to bed can disturb your sleep.

Your mind will continue to process these external stimuli, making it hard for you to relax and fall asleep. Therefore, it's better to remove the clutter from your bedroom to promote a night of peaceful and comfortable sleep.

4. Eliminates allergens in your home

According to the Centers for Disease Control and Prevention, during the year 2021, about 25.7% of grown-ups experienced seasonal allergies, 7.3% suffered from eczema, and 6.2% had food allergies. Allergy symptoms can vary from mild symptoms like watery eyes and itching to severe reactions like anaphylaxis, which can be life-threatening. Allergies can significantly affect a person's quality of life.

Dirt, animal fur, and plant pollen tend to accumulate in various areas of a home. Therefore, keeping unused items in your home will only lead to clutter, dust build-up, and allergens.

It is crucial to declutter all the rooms in your house, including those that are not frequently used, like the attic. The dust particles in such areas can circulate and reach other rooms, resulting in poor indoor air quality.

Therefore, reducing clutter can help enhance your home's air circulation. This enhancement will benefit family members or friends who have allergies, hay fever, asthma, or eczema, as they will experience a significant improvement in their symptoms.

5. More space at your home.

Decluttering your home can result in the creation of more physical space. By only keeping the items you love, value, and appreciate, you can eliminate the accumulation of unnecessary and random clutter that might be taking up space in various areas, such as cupboards, drawers, shelves, work surfaces, and even on the floor and stairs.

Removing clutter can help you optimize the available space in your home, regardless of its size. Furthermore, it can improve the flow of movement within your home and provide a clearer line of sight from one room to another, giving the impression of more space and making it easier for you to move around and enjoy your living area.

6. Ease in finding your stuff

Are you constantly losing something? Where do you put your glasses when you come home? Do you have a box full of socks, but none have pairs?

If you have fewer possessions, it's less likely that you will misplace something, and it will be easier to locate items. In addition, with less clutter, you find things more efficiently.

As you declutter and decide what to keep and discard, you will likely reorganize your belongings and establish proper storage, filing systems, and designated places for items. Consequently, you will better understand where everything is, making it easier to locate your possessions.

7. You develop your home style.

When you declutter your belongings, you keep certain items and eliminate others. This action can help you identify patterns and themes in your style. For instance, you may prefer neutral colors in your clothing and decor while avoiding bold patterns and bright colors.

Through the process of decluttering, you can gain a better understanding of your style, which can be helpful when making future purchasing decisions. For example, instead of making impulsive purchases based on sales and discounts, you can be more intentional and selective in your buying choices based on needs and preferences.

Now, let me share a story of a previously stressed-out mom who needed inspiration to change her home lifestyle.

As a mother of two small kids, Hannah used to feel constantly overwhelmed with a never-ending to-do list. Whenever she tried to spend time with her children playing games or coloring, her mind would be preoccupied with everything she had to manage. Sad to say, she could not fully enjoy the moment.

One day, her two-year-old had a tantrum and yelled, "Stop it!" It made her realize that he had learned this behavior from her, and she felt angry at herself for the level of anxiety she was experiencing every day.

She wanted to create a peaceful, calm environment for her children to learn and grow. She needed to make some changes to reduce her stress levels.

Initially, she joined a decluttering course out of curiosity, the need for concrete steps, and a support system to help with the process. Even though she had already done some cleaning alone, the course and community were life-changing for her in the best ways possible.

By following the course guidelines, she simplified her life and became aware of other things. For example, her learned strategies helped her change her mindset from an anxious and depressed mom to someone present and calm while spending time with her children.

Like Hannah, you can also benefit from decluttering your home. Whatever your specific needs are, the process can only brighten your daily home experience.

Chapter Two: Getting Started: Preparing Your Mind and Space

No, goals are not your dreams. A goal is something to which you put all your efforts and energy into achieving your objectives.

Goals are like a map that guides you toward a specific destination. This sense of direction provides enthusiasm, inspiration, additional vigor, and a purpose to start your day. Consequently, you feel more invigorated and animated.

Goals are essential because they give you a sense of direction. You know where you are going if you have a clear path causing fewer stressors and pressures in life. This way, you don't spend time wandering and making no progress.

Having goals provides motivation and adds excitement to life. Having a precise aim gives a sense of direction and purpose, which boosts your happiness, confidence, and sense of security.

For instance, someone to lose 10 pounds in two months is more motivated to exercise regularly and eat healthily than someone with no weight loss goal.

Goals also enhance focus and eliminate distractions. By setting clear objectives, you can concentrate on the things that matter most, avoiding unproductive or irrelevant activities. For example, a student who aims to get an A grade in math will prioritize studying and doing math-related exercises over spending time on other leisure activities.

Without goals, you may lack a sense of direction and drift from one thing to another without any intention of accomplishment. For instance, someone with no career aspirations might switch jobs frequently without building valuable skills or expertise. As a result, they may need help to achieve meaningful success in their chosen field.

An airplane has a set route it has to follow to arrive at its destination. So does a ship. Wind and weather conditions can affect the airplane's and ship's courses. However, knowing the exact destination enables the pilot and the captain to make the proper adjustments. So, it is with goals.

Having goals for having a clean and beautiful home can make maintaining a tidy and organized living space much easier and more enjoyable. Setting specific objectives, such as decluttering a particular room, creating a cleaning schedule, or implementing a home decor plan, can provide direction and motivation.

Goals can also prioritize tasks and make it easier to track progress, allowing for a greater sense of accomplishment and satisfaction. It is better to have a simple or not-so-important goal than to have no goals at all.

Now, let me ask - What are your goals?

The Preparation

As Athena started to declutter her home, she experienced a distressing sensation.

"I know I need to declutter but lack the necessary skills and knowledge. This task is way too challenging," she told herself.

This thinking would often lead to procrastination, resulting in disorganization in her life. It felt too overwhelming for her to tackle the task.

However, she thankfully called up a friend who told her she needed a bit of preparation. But, of course, it's always best to be "ready" for this task.

After trying what her friend recommended, Athena felt rejuvenated, prouder, and lighter. Maintaining organization is critical in everyone's life, and having someone and some things to assist you through the process can make the task less burdensome.

Decluttering can be a demanding and draining task. But if you are well-prepared for it, you can win over any struggles.

Before beginning the decluttering process, taking a few essential steps to simplify your home and life is crucial. These preparatory actions will enable you to declutter more efficiently and streamline the process, resulting in a more effective outcome. In addition, they will help you achieve optimal results from your decluttering efforts and clear out the clutter timelier and efficiently.

Here are those steps:

1. Determine the reason why you are decluttering.

Before starting the decluttering process, it is essential to clarify the reason or motivation behind it. This reason, also known as your "why," will serve as a guiding principle to help you determine what items to keep and what to discard.

- Do you want a more organized living space?
- Will someone be moving into the house?
- Do you want to relieve yourself of stress?
- Do you want to save money?
- Do you want to turn your back on the past?
- Are you creating a more aesthetically pleasing home?

These are some of the many questions you can ask yourself to prepare for the task. By understanding your why, you can identify which possessions bring value to your life and which merely add to the chaos and distractions.

The more clarity you have regarding your reason or motivation for decluttering, the better equipped you will be to simplify and organize your home.

2. Create a plan

Creating a plan for decluttering is recommended as it can assist you in organizing the various aspects of the process before initiating it. Additionally, it can aid in anticipating and preventing common obstacles that may arise during decluttering, which could impede your progress and unnecessarily complicate the task.

There's a four-step process to your planning.

The initial step in creating a decluttering plan is determining "When." Next, it would help you to decide whether you want to declutter in longer sessions, shorter intervals, or a mix of both. Once you have chosen, schedule the decluttering sessions in your calendar and commit yourself to following them.

The second one is the "How." Various decluttering methods are available, each with its advantages and disadvantages. The critical factor is determining which approach aligns with your schedule, preferences, lifestyle, and objectives.

For instance, consider whether you want to declutter room by room or by category of items. Additionally, determine whether you'll tackle most of the decluttering alone or with the assistance of your family or a professional person who declutters.

The third is "Were." Establish a designated area to temporarily store items you plan to discard or sell while awaiting your next trip to the donation center. Locating this holding area in a convenient yet discreet spot is advisable to avoid tempting yourself or your family to rummage through the items and undo your decluttering progress.

Additionally, I recommend boxing or bagging the items beforehand. The purpose is to minimize the possibility of second-guessing your decluttering decisions or needing help transporting the items to the donation center.

The fourth and final one is "What." Another crucial aspect of your decluttering plan is determining the course of action for the items you wish to dispose of. Again, allocate a few minutes beforehand to determine where you'll donate the items or attempt to sell them to avoid any inconvenience.

Be aware of the donation centers you intend to use for your items, their operating hours, and the items they accept. If you plan to sell any items, decide on your method and platform, such as Facebook Marketplace or Craigslist, hosting a yard sale, etc.

3. Set the right expectation.

Setting reasonable and achievable objectives can help keep you motivated and optimistic throughout decluttering. Consider your time and energy constraints when establishing decluttering goals and develop practical timelines accordingly. Remember that specific spaces and types of possessions might be more challenging to declutter than others, so adjust your expectations accordingly.

Decluttering your entire home is a process that takes time and effort but rather a gradual and continuous one. Recognizing this and setting practical expectations can help you feel more accomplished and motivated to keep going.

4. Perform a decluttering sweep.

A brief initial scan is helpful before beginning decluttering in a particular space. Look for things that are easy to dispose of, such as trash, superficial clutter, or decorative objects you do not like or cherish, and eliminate them immediately.

Gather things in a box or basket while searching for anything that belongs in other rooms or needs to be elsewhere. You can use this basket to collect items that require relocation as you declutter, and you can put them away later when you have finished decluttering for the day.

5. Collect the necessary tools and materials for decluttering.

To make decluttering easier and more efficient, you don't need much. However, I recommend having a few bags, boxes, or baskets for different categories, such as items you plan to sell, items to donate, garbage, and things that belong in other areas of the house.

Bringing a water bottle, drink, and snack can help you stay energized. You may also want to listen to music or a podcast to make the process more enjoyable.

Now, you are good to go!

Getting started with decluttering can be challenging as it may seem overwhelming to tackle a whole house, or you may need help with where to begin without feeling like you're progressing. However, once you take the

first steps and start decluttering, the process becomes much easier, and you will likely find it easier to continue.

With that in mind, I am leaving you with motivational quotes and affirmations. They will help you eliminate overwhelming and negative thoughts and can inspire and guide you.

You can either use the affirmations provided as they are or make adjustments to make them more personal and meaningful to you. Most importantly, your commitments and promises should align with your beliefs and values and feel authentic.

I can exercise the necessary discipline and endurance to undertake this decluttering endeavor gradually and steadily.

Cleaning brings me tranquility and a sense of calm.

I maintain a systematic arrangement of my workspace and documents, allowing me to finish assignments promptly.

I can make sound choices concerning my possessions, acquisitions, and obligations.

I enjoy living an organized, clutter-free life.

I am organized and efficient.

I organize every area of my life.

Living in an orderly and clutter-free environment is something I find pleasurable.

I am grateful for the energy I possess.

The tasks I undertake are well-arranged and enjoyable to complete.

I appreciate my ability to maximize my resources to the fullest.

Being systematic and competent comes naturally to me. I have clear goals and know how to achieve them.

I am content with maintaining order and neatness in my life.

Every aspect of my existence is meticulously arranged and orderly.

Chapter Three: Decluttering Techniques: Letting Go of Unnecessary Items

Dianne had always been a sentimental person. She treasured every memory, every moment, and every item that had a special place in her heart. Dianne filled her home with mementos from her childhood, teenage years, and married life. She keeps stuff from her children's younger days. She couldn't bear to let go of anything, especially her kids' old clothes, toys, and books.

Dianne's husband, Sam, had been trying to convince her to declutter their home for years, but she always found an excuse to keep everything. She had convinced herself that these items held sentimental value and were part of her family's history. She felt that one day, her grandchildren would cherish them too. But, her cluttered home was causing stress and anxiety for everyone, especially Dianne.

One day, Dianne's son, Geoff, visited her with his wife and two kids. As soon as they entered the house, Dianne felt ashamed of the mess and clutter surrounding her. She tried to make excuses for the piles of stuff, but her daughter-in-law, Carla, gently said, "Mom, we don't need all these things to remember the good times we had. We have our memories.

At first, Dianne felt defensive, but then she looked around and realized that she had been holding on to things that were no longer necessary. While focusing on preserving the past, she still needs to enjoy the present. In addition, she realized that her family was more important than all the clutter in her home.

Over the next few days, Dianne went through every room in the house and began sorting out items. It was hard at first, but she felt a sense of liberation as she continued. Finally, she let go of old clothes, broken toys, and knick-knacks that had been collecting dust for years.

As Dianne cleared the clutter, she felt a sense of peace she hadn't experienced in years. She found joy in her created space and felt lighter and happier. She realized the cherished memories were not in the items but in the moments, she had shared with her family.

Ultimately, Dianne donated most of the items to charity and kept only a few extraordinary things to her. Nevertheless, she felt a sense of accomplishment and knew her family would appreciate the changes she had made. She also knew she had set an excellent example for her children and grandchildren.

From that day forward, Dianne promised to live in the present and cherish the moments she shared with her family. She realized that holding on to unnecessary items only created clutter and stress. She learned that the most essential things in life were the people she loved, not the things she owned.

The Art of Letting Go

Decluttering is more than just clearing away junk. It often entails parting ways with valuable, costly, prized possessions, and it signifies relinquishing exceptional items in pursuit of something more significant.

Yes, it's easier said than done. How can a mother let go of the gown her firstborn wore when she brought him home from the hospital?

But once you realize the greater purpose of what you are doing, it will be easy. Anyway, you can turn to these tips:

1. Change your perspective.

Your perception of decluttering can significantly influence your motivation to engage in it. For example, it will not be a pleasant endeavor if you view it as an obligatory burden, a task that will consume considerable time and effort. However, altering your perspective and considering it a chance to streamline your life can become a much more favorable experience.

Consider the numerous advantages of decluttering: reduced stress, increased tranquility, and a more uncomplicated existence. When you begin to recognize the positives, it becomes easier to release the negatives.

2. Don't look at the past. Focus on the future.

Many individuals cling to belongings because they fear detaching themselves from the past. We may hold on to clothes we wore in high school or keepsakes from childhood.

While it's natural to desire to keep these items, it's essential to recognize that they are merely material possessions. They do not determine your identity as an individual.

If you find it challenging to let go of the past, try focusing on the future instead. What kind of life do you envision in 5, 10, or even 20 years? Do you wish to be burdened by many belongings, or would you prefer to travel light and savor life?

3. Ignore the guilt trip.

Guilt often accompanies the process of decluttering. For example, we frequently experience guilt when we consider getting rid of something gifted to us, or we may feel wasteful for discarding certain items.

However, there's an important realization: you should not feel guilty about decluttering. It's your life, and you can live it according to your preferences.

If guilt arises while decluttering, remind yourself that the person who gave you the item would want you to be happy. They wouldn't want you to hold onto something that doesn't bring you joy.

4. Think of the saying, "It's better to give than to receive."

The act of giving a gift is to bring happiness to the recipient. You can focus on that. Instead of thinking that you will be letting go of the precious toys your kids adored, focus on the happiness you will bring if you donate them.

Decluttering does not mean you are throwing stuff away. You can donate your items to the community. For example, offer books to schools and libraries as donations. Provide clothing and other household items to your area's local foster care organizations, shelters, and food pantries.

5. Disregard thoughts of money.

Although it may be challenging, attempting to detach yourself from the money you invested in an item when decluttering is crucial. The temptation to hold onto something can arise because you feel like you wasted money on it, but such thinking is unproductive.

Remember, material possessions are precisely that: material. They do not define your worth, nor do they determine your happiness.

6. Visualize your desired outcomes.

Reflect on the reasons behind your desire to declutter. Then, imagine a tranquil, inviting, and clutter-free environment within your home, and visualize the experience of returning to such a place.

You may even consider crafting an inspiration board or assembling a collection on Pinterest that showcases images reminiscent of the space you aim to create. When you devote time to your objectives, you often ignite your motivation to part with your belongings.

7. Acknowledge that the item has fulfilled its purpose.

It's acceptable to express gratitude for that item and then let go. As stated by Marie Kondo, "To truly cherish the things that are important to you, you must first discard those that have outlived their purpose. To throw away what you no longer need is neither wasteful nor shameful."

When struggling to let go of an item, an important question is whether it has served its intended function. For instance, what do you do if you have an expensive ball gown you wore to a party that no longer fits you and will most likely never wear again? Recognizing that an item has fulfilled its purpose and is no longer necessary will make it easier to part with it.

It's important to note that deciding what to keep and what to give away is a personal choice. Giving away unnecessary possessions and releasing attachments can bring incredible blessings to your living space and overall life. Although it may be challenging, the rewards of this effort can be significant. Creating a room in your home allows you to appreciate and be thankful for what you already have, leading to fulfillment.

A Clutter-Free Environment

Productivity and creativity are two of the most important benefits of a clutter-free environment.

How does it affect productivity? Let's face it; all this clutter distracts you.

The human brain has a limited ability to handle information. So although you may think the presence of used coffee cups and piles of books on your desk is unimportant, they distract you, whether you're aware of it.

When numerous visual distractions vie for your attention simultaneously, it becomes difficult to concentrate on the task you're working on. So, it's either you do very little or nothing at all.

You may be working on an overdue report, and still, you cannot begin since, for the past hour, you have been distracted by the pen holder on your desk. It is overflowing because you have not even removed the ones that have run out of ink!

You may be getting ready for work in the morning, but your bedroom is cluttered with clothes, shoes, and accessories scattered over the floor and furniture. As a result, precious minutes slip away as you search for a specific outfit or accessory, causing unnecessary stress and potential delay in doing your tasks at the office.

This situation disrupts your morning routine and sets a chaotic tone for the rest of the day, affecting your overall productivity. By decluttering your home and establishing organized systems, such as designated storage spaces for belongings, you can streamline your routines, save time, and create a more conducive environment for productivity and well-being.

How does clutter affect your creativity?

"Clutter is not my friend; it is my enemy." That's what Jeff Goins said in his article "Clutter Is Killing Your Creativity (And What to Do About It)."

He also said that clutter:

- Encourages procrastination
- Is a form of resistance
- Is a form of self-sabotage
- Keeps you from creating worthwhile and vital stuff.

Clutter has a profound effect on our ability to maintain focus. When our physical surroundings are disorganized and cluttered, our minds become overwhelmed and easily distracted. In addition, the presence of visual stimuli competing for our attention diverts our focus from the task at hand.

Focus and creativity are connected and provide the necessary concentration and mental clarity to delve deep into a task or problem, creating the ability to generate unique and innovative ideas. By honing our focus, we can better channel our creative energies, enabling us to explore new perspectives, make connections, and think outside the box, leading to enhanced creative output and problem-solving capabilities.

If you are working on a new art project, you need to tap into your creativity. So, you need to focus. By decluttering your workspace at home, you can enhance your focus. This focused state allows you to immerse yourself in the artistic process, explore different techniques, and unleash your creative expression, resulting in a masterpiece that reflects your unique vision and artistic abilities.

Clutter can negatively impact the aspect of imagination or brainstorming. It creates a chaotic and visually overwhelming environment that stifles creative thinking and hinders new ideas.

For example, a writer attempts to brainstorm ideas for a novel in a cluttered study. The scattered papers, books, and miscellaneous items create a visual distraction that disrupts the writer's thought process. The clutter becomes a barrier to free-flowing creativity, making exploring fresh concepts and developing innovative storylines challenging. By creating an organized and clutter-free workspace, the writer can eliminate distractions, clear mental space, and foster a conducive environment for creative imagination.

Creativity and productivity are vital because they contribute to personal development and success in various areas of life. Creativity fuels innovative ideas and unique approaches, while productivity ensures efficient execution, leading to tangible outcomes.

In her blog, Micheline talks about how every time she has to declutter, whenever she moves apartments, or when that time she has to sell her mother's house, the process takes an emotional toll on her.

Regret. Nostalgia. Sometimes, unexplainable feelings pop up.

Suddenly, recollections of the day she purchased or received a gift from someone resurfaced. Regarding her mother, vivid images emerged of various locations where she proudly sported one of her extensive collections of 60 pairs of shoes, diligently stored in their original boxes with each shoe meticulously wrapped in tissue paper.

However, she has also gained valuable insights about letting go of precious stuff. One of the most important is that she needs to look at things as things. Whenever she attempts to pack away something, she thinks of the associated person: her best friend who gave her the stuffed animal or her mother who wore the shoes. As soon as she learned this lesson, each process became more manageable.

Releasing your grip on non-essential belongings is a liberating act. By letting go of material possessions that no longer serve a purpose or hold sentimental value, one can experience a newfound sense of freedom and lightness.

Chapter Four: Cleaning Techniques: Creating a Clean and Healthy Home

Maintaining a clean house is of utmost importance for several reasons. Firstly, a clean house promotes physical health and well-being. Regular cleaning and tidying up helps eliminate dust, allergens, and harmful bacteria that can accumulate on surfaces, leading to respiratory issues, allergies, and other health problems. A clean home provides a healthier environment for everyone living in it, reducing the risk of illnesses and improving overall quality of life.

Secondly, a clean house has a positive impact on mental health. A messy living area can create feelings of stress, anxiety, and being overwhelmed. Meanwhile, a clean and organized environment promotes a sense of calmness and order, which can contribute to improved mental well-being. In addition, a tidy home allows for better focus, productivity, and relaxation, making it easier to unwind and enjoy time spent at home.

Furthermore, a clean house fosters a sense of pride and satisfaction. Coming home to a clean and well-maintained living space can boost one's mood and create a sense of accomplishment. In addition, it reflects personal responsibility and respect for oneself and others. A clean house is also more inviting and welcoming, making it a pleasant space for hosting guests and spending quality time with family and friends.

Overall, maintaining a clean house goes beyond just appearances. It is crucial in supporting physical and mental well-being and creating a harmonious and enjoyable living environment.

Exploring Effective and Efficient Cleaning Techniques

Maintaining a beautiful, comfortable home requires more than stylish decor and cozy furniture. It also entails a regular and thorough cleaning regimen to ensure a pristine living environment. Delve into the realm of effective and efficient cleaning techniques that can help you achieve a clean home while optimizing your time and energy.

While a tidy and organized home certainly brings aesthetic satisfaction, the key objective is to create a safe and healthy living environment. Regular cleaning practices such as dusting, mopping, and disinfecting surfaces help eliminate harmful allergens, dust mites, and bacteria that can cause respiratory issues and allergies. By focusing on the well-being of the occupants, a clean house becomes a sanctuary that promotes physical health and contributes to a higher quality of life.

Here are some practical tips when cleaning different areas of your home.

Let's start with the kitchen.

A spotless kitchen is essential for several reasons. Firstly, it ensures food safety by preventing the spread of harmful bacteria and contaminants that can cause foodborne illnesses. Maintaining cleanliness reduces the risk of cross-contamination and promotes a hygienic environment for food preparation.

Secondly, a clean kitchen enables efficient and enjoyable cooking. A clutter-free and organized space allows easy access to ingredients and utensils, streamlining the cooking process. In addition, a spotless kitchen enhances the cooking experience by eliminating unpleasant odors and creating a welcoming atmosphere providing a pleasant environment.

How to clean kitchen surfaces:

1. Wash your hands with soap and water for 20 seconds before you touch anything, especially if you've been outside or at work.

2. Make it a habit to clean various kitchen surfaces consistently, such as countertops, tabletops, and frequently touched areas like stove or microwave controls. If possible, opt for a disinfectant approved by the Environmental Protection Agency (EPA).

3. Wash all dishes and silverware before and after you use them.

4. Clean and store sponges correctly so they won't harbor mold, germs, and foodborne pathogens. Here are some techniques to ensure your sponges are germ-free.

a) One effective method to clean a sponge is placing it in the dishwasher with a high-temperature setting and using the drying cycle.

b) Another way to sanitize a sponge is by wetting it and microwaving it for 1-2 minutes.

To prevent mold and bacteria growth, it is vital to squeeze out the sponge well after each use and store it in a location that allows for proper air drying.

Cloth dish towels solely used for drying clean dishes can still harbor harmful microorganisms. To ensure the towels' cleanliness, I recommend washing them frequently using your washing machine's hot temperature.

Are you a regular fixture in your kitchen? Do you like preparing your food from scratch? If that's the case, you may use your chopping board often.

To prevent cross-contamination and the potential spread of harmful bacteria like salmonella and E. coli, avoiding using the same cutting board for fruits/vegetables and raw meat is essential. Before switching, it is best to clean the cutting board with hot water and soap. Having separate cutting boards, one dedicated to raw meat and the other for fruits, vegetables, and other items, is a wise practice.

Let's move into the bedroom.

The bedroom is a serene sanctuary that unveils a world of solace and rejuvenation. So, pay special attention to cleanliness in your most sacred place.

Dust mites are unwelcome bed companions that contribute to decreased air quality and have the potential to cause discomfort, regardless of one's allergy status.

Here are a few suggestions for eliminating dust mites:

1. Utilize mattress and pillow covers made of plastic with zippered closures.

2. Every week, launder all bedding using hot water at temperatures exceeding 130°F to eliminate dust mites effectively.

3. Consistently vacuum mattresses that are not covered to remove dust mites.

Do you have messy rooms in your house? Here's an organized method for making them tidy:

1. Dispose of the trash.

First, prioritize discarding the food wrappers, empty snack containers, unwanted shopping bags, and junk mail to improve the room's appearance effortlessly. Next, consider setting a timer and observing how much trash you can identify within a brief timeframe. Achieving quick progress will inspire you to continue your efforts.

2. Take out the belongings that are clearly out of place in the room.

Is the vacuum standing in the middle of the floor? Store it in the closet!

Kitchen scissors on your dresser? Please put it back inside the kitchen drawer!

Are dirty clothes scattered everywhere? Gather everything and put it in the laundry room!

By scanning areas frequently, you will see items you can remove from the room without significant consideration. This scanning is a fundamental "grab-and-go" step before initiating any sorting and organizing tasks.

3.   Remember to dust!

You can ensure that you are wiping all your furniture thoroughly, including dressers, bed frames, and nightstands; you should use a damp cloth. A damp cloth is more effective than a dry cloth because of the scientific principle of capillary force.

A damp cloth creates capillary action that attracts and lifts dust particles instead of merely spreading them around. The wet cloth draws in the particles and effectively removes dust from the surface.

After the damp cloth, take another clean cloth or paper towel moistened with soapy water to clean these surfaces again, then rinse off with plain water. Also, remember to pay attention to ceiling fans as they accumulate dirt quickly due to periodic cleaning.

Additionally, make sure to move furniture away from the floor. This action will allow you to eliminate all those bothersome dust bunnies hiding under tables or chairs that are only usually visible by lifting the furniture.

4.   Window Cleaning

Remember to clean your windows. It is essential to clean them at least once a month or more frequently. Utilize a glass cleaner and a cloth that does not produce lint to clean your bedroom's interior and exterior windowpanes.

If you encounter challenging spots or stubborn dirt, you may choose a mixture of vinegar and water as an alternative solution. Take care not to apply excessive pressure while cleaning the windows, which can result in streaks. Instead, gently wipe across the surface in a single direction for optimal outcomes.

If you have curtains or drapes, remove them before cleaning. Then, you can put them back or, if it's time, put on new ones.

5. Change bedroom linen

It is advisable to replace your bed linens every few weeks, depending on their frequency of use. This practice helps to prevent the accumulation of dust mites.

Neglecting dust mites can lead to allergic reactions, particularly in the summer when airborne allergens are more prevalent. It's crucial to ensure that everything is adequately dried before storing it, as failure may result in mold growth on the fabric.

Let's go to the bathroom.

It is essential to be thorough in cleaning the bathroom for several reasons:

1. The bathroom is where germs and bacteria can thrive, so a thorough cleaning helps maintain hygiene and prevent the spread of illness.

2. The bathroom is often exposed to moisture, which creates an ideal environment for the growth of mold and mildew.

3. Keeping the bathroom clean and well-maintained can enhance the overall appearance and comfort of the space.

You can achieve quick and effective bathroom cleaning by adhering to the following steps:

1. Empty all areas of the bathroom.

To optimize efficiency, perform this task for the entire bathroom at once rather than in stages. Take out all shower and bathtub products. Place used towels and rugs outside the room. Transfer any items from the counters to a location outside the bathroom. Remember also to collect any trash cans.

2. Apply a cleaner on the shower area and the sink.

If you clean your shower regularly, use an all-purpose cleaner. However, if you're dealing with stubborn buildup, opt for an acid-based cleaner. If applicable, ensure you apply the cleaner to the shower track and inside the shower door. Then, allow it to soak and work its magic.

3. Do the same in other areas.

Apply the all-purpose cleaner onto your chosen cleaning tool, such as a microfiber cloth or sponge. Then, wipe down shelves, towel racks, doors, baseboards, blinds, and windowsills. You should work in sections, starting from the top of the room and moving downwards from left to right.

4. Sanitize the toilet.

If you frequently scrub the interior of your toilet, using an all-purpose cleaner should be sufficient. Apply the cleaner to the inside of the toilet bowl and clean with a toilet brush before flushing.

You can use a specialized toilet cleaner by spraying or sprinkling it for any stubborn buildup. Afterward, spray the exterior of the toilet with the all-purpose cleaner and wipe it clean using a cloth.

5. Mop the floor.

Dip your mop into the cleaning solution bucket, wring out any excess water, and clean the bathroom floor. After the floor has dried, place the trash can back in its position and put your recently washed rugs back in place.

Let's attack the floors.

In high-traffic sections like kitchens, dining areas, bathrooms, entryways, and hallways, sweep or vacuum the floors every one to three days and mop them once a week. Regularly cleaning or vacuuming is crucial to preserve the flooring's finish and longevity, as it eliminates dirt and debris that can harm the floor from foot traffic.

Here is a step-by-step guide to cleaning the floor:

1. Select a mop and buckets.

When choosing a mop, it's essential to consider the type of floor you have. The traditional string or strip mop is best for textured floors like ceramic tiles. On the other hand, if you have a smooth base, a sponge mop will be suitable. Mop buckets with built-in wringers are ideal for string or strip mops, while any bucket with a handle will suffice for a sponge mop.

2. Select a cleaner.

Floors may need a specific type of cleaning fluid. It's advisable to avoid products marketed as "mop and shine," as these can result in a buildup that eventually causes yellowing over time.

3. Sweep or vacuum.

Before starting the mopping process, it's essential to thoroughly sweep or vacuum the floor to prevent it from becoming sticky or muddy. This step is also an opportunity to pre-clean any damp or dirty areas you come across while sweeping or vacuuming. You can accomplish this using a sponge with soapy water or a suitable household cleaning solution. Make sure that it is safe for your specific flooring.

4. Prepare the buckets.

Begin by filling each bucket with hot water, as it is more effective and efficient for cleaning than cold or warm water. Next, add the appropriate amount of mopping detergent to the wash bucket. It's essential to resist the urge to use more detergent to enhance cleaning effectiveness or speed up the process. I don't recommend this. Instead, always adhere to the instructions provided on the detergent label.

5. Dip and squeeze the mop.

Immerse your mop into the bucket and remove excess water using a wringer or manually wringing it out. The mop should be slightly damp rather than excessively wet. Excessive water dripping from the mop can cause damage to the floor and significantly prolong the drying process.

6. Start mopping.

You can start from one end and gradually progress to the other end. Move backward so you always stand on a floor that needs mopping. Prevent tracks or footprints using a sponge mop in straight lines. For rag mops, employ a figure-8 motion to optimize the mop's design and effectiveness.

7. Address stubborn spots.

Take a moment to focus on those areas. Then, apply firm downward pressure and vigorously rub back and forth over the spot to eliminate the grime. For corners and edges that are difficult to reach, you may need to squat down and scrub the floor using a sponge or paper towel. This targeted approach ensures thorough cleaning in problematic areas.

8. Rinse the mopped section.

Once you have finished scrubbing a small area of the floor, it is important to rinse your mop properly in the rinse bucket. First, submerge the mop in the water and move it up and down a few times to ensure thorough rinsing. Afterward, wring out the mop to eliminate as much dirty water from the mop head as you can. This step maintains the cleanliness of the mop.

A gentle reminder -

Using non-toxic products in cleaning the house is essential for several reasons. Firstly, it promotes a healthier living environment by minimizing exposure to harmful chemicals irritating the skin, eyes, and respiratory system. Secondly, it helps protect the overall ecosystem by reducing pollution and preventing the release of hazardous substances into water sources and the atmosphere.

Using cleaning supplies or household products can lead to various health issues like eye and throat irritation, headaches, and respiratory problems. In addition, volatile organic compounds (VOCs) in many cleaning products can vaporize at room temperature and release hazardous chemicals.

Before purchasing cleaning supplies and household products, it is essential to read and review all labels carefully. Then, opt for products that are either free of or have minimized levels of volatile organic compounds (VOCs), fragrances, irritants, and flammable ingredients.

Keeping a clean home is not just about tidiness; it reflects the positive energy and peace we invite into our lives. Maintaining a clean and organized space creates an environment that nurtures our physical and mental well-being.

Embrace cleanliness by envisioning the benefits it brings. A clean home offers a sanctuary to relax, think clearly, and recharge energy. It promotes productivity, reduces stress, and enhances overall happiness.

You deserve a clean and inviting space and commit to the daily actions that will help you achieve it. Remember, your effort to maintain a clean home is an investment in yourself and your overall quality of life.

Chapter Five: Designing Your Dream Home: Creating a Beautiful and Cozy Space

In homeownership, few endeavors are as thrilling and fulfilling as designing your dream home. It is an opportunity to translate your unique vision into reality, shaping a living space that perfectly encapsulates your style, personality, and comfort. With every aspect customizable, from the architectural layout to the finest interior design details, creating a beautiful and cozy space becomes an artistic journey like no other.

Your journey begins with envisioning a home that reflects your aesthetic preferences and embraces the essence of coziness. A beautiful home is not solely defined by its appearance but also by its sense of warmth and comfort. From the selection of color palettes to the choice of furniture and home decor, every element plays a pivotal role in cultivating an inviting ambiance. Whether you prefer a rustic farmhouse retreat or a sleek modern oasis, designing your dream home enables you to weave together aesthetics and functionality, creating a space that harmoniously balances beauty and comfort.

Vision to Reality

A friend of mine had always dreamed of creating a perfect home - one she had dreamed of ever since she was a little girl.

Brimming with vibrant colors, innovative layouts, and unique home decor ideas and with unwavering determination, Emily embarked on a journey to turn her vision into a reality.

Emily meticulously sketched her dream home on countless pages, blending contemporary elegance with a touch of rustic charm. She imagined an open concept living space flooded with natural light, adorned with sleek furniture and decorated walls that would serve as a canvas for her eclectic art collection.

With her design plans solid, Emily began searching for the ideal location. Finally, stumbling upon a picturesque plot of land nestled amidst rolling hills, Emily knew she had found the perfect place to embrace nature's beauty.

Drawing inspiration from the surrounding landscape, Emily incorporated large windows throughout the house to invite breathtaking views inside. She handpicked sustainable materials, blending them seamlessly to create an eco-friendly haven. Every detail, from the mosaic tile backsplash in the kitchen to the cozy reading nook by the window, was thoughtfully curated to reflect her personality.

The journey was not without its challenges. Emily faced setbacks, budget constraints, and unexpected delays. Yet, she remained steadfast in her pursuit of perfection. She poured her heart and soul into each decision, knowing the result would be worth it.

Weeks turned into months as Emily's dream home gradually took shape. Painted in vibrant hues, carefully selected furniture pieces found their place, and the air filled with the scent of fresh flowers and the soft glow of carefully placed lighting created a warm and inviting atmosphere.

Finally, the day arrived when Emily stood in the doorway of her dream home, tears of joy streaming down her face. The vision that once lived solely in her imagination now stood before her, a testament to her passion and dedication.

With her heart full of gratitude, Emily stepped inside, ready to embrace the haven she had created. Finally, her dream had become reality, a sanctuary that would inspire her creativity and welcome her home with open arms.

Designing a home is an opportunity to unleash your creativity and transform your living space into a true reflection of yourself. You can infuse your unique style and personality into every nook and cranny with each design choice.

Do you want to have the same journey as Emily? Do you want to design the home of your dreams?

Let's first talk about having a cohesive design.

Cohesion plays a vital role in interior design as it encompasses visual appeal and the creation of a welcoming and balanced ambiance. When your living space exhibits a cohesive look, it not only pleases the eye but also fosters a comfortable atmosphere that draws you in. By placing importance on cohesion in your design choices, you can achieve a seamlessly integrated appearance for your home.

Creating a cohesive design style is essential to achieving a harmonious and visually pleasing aesthetic in your home. Here are some critical steps to help you achieve a cohesive design style:

1. Define your design style

Start by identifying the design style that most resonates with you, whether modern, traditional, farmhouse, minimalist, or eclectic. Clearly understanding your preferred style will serve as a guiding principle throughout the design process.

2. Establish a color palette.

Select a color palette that compliments your chosen design style. Consider mixing primary and accent colors to create depth and visual interest. Stick to a consistent color scheme throughout your home to maintain a cohesive look.

3. Have consistent materials and textures.

Choose materials and textures that are consistent with your design style. For example, if you prefer a rustic farmhouse style, incorporate natural materials like wood, stone, and textured fabrics. Consistency in materials and textures will tie different elements of your home together.

4. Balance proportions and scale.

Pay attention to the proportions and scale of furniture and decor items in each room. Ensure that they are in harmony with the size of the space and with each other.

A balanced arrangement of furniture and appropriately scaled decor will contribute to a cohesive overall design.

For instance, imagine you have a small bedroom with a low ceiling. To create a balanced aesthetic, opt for appropriately scaled furniture, such as a compact platform bed with a streamlined frame. Pair it with a smaller nightstand and a slender floor lamp to maintain proportionality.

Additionally, consider using vertical elements like a tall, slim mirror or floor-to-ceiling curtains to draw the eye upward and create an illusion of height. By carefully selecting furniture and incorporating vertical elements, you can achieve a balanced composition that maximizes the available space and creates a visually pleasing atmosphere.

5. Pay attention to details.

Consider the more minor details, such as lighting fixtures, hardware, and accessories. These elements can significantly influence the overall design style. Make sure they align with your chosen aesthetic and complement the other design elements in your home.

6. Create a visual flow.

Establish a sense of continuity and flow between rooms. Use elements like color, patterns, and materials to connect different spaces.

Consistent flooring or wall treatments can also help create a seamless transition from one area to another.

For example, imagine a home where the living room, dining area, and kitchen share an open floor plan. You can choose a neutral color scheme of soft grays and whites to establish visual flow. In the living room, incorporate a gray sofa with white accent chairs while using light gray walls and white trim. Moving into the dining area, continue the color scheme with a white table and gray upholstered chairs. Finally, hang a modern chandelier with silver accents above the table to complement the overall design.

In the kitchen, maintain a consistent color palette using white cabinetry, gray subway tiles for the backsplash, and white quartz countertops. Using a consistent color palette throughout these spaces creates a sense of unity and flow, allowing the eye to move seamlessly from one room to another.

7. Edit and simplify.

Finally, remember that less can be enough when creating a cohesive design style. Avoid clutter and excessive ornamentation. Instead, choose to include only the elements contributing to the overall design concept, ensuring a clean and cohesive look.

Following these steps and staying true to your chosen design style, you can create a cohesive and visually appealing home that reflects your taste and preferences.

What about choosing the right furniture and decor pieces? Let me help you with that.

1. First, you need to pick a theme.

Which sounds good to you?

- contemporary (featuring metallic and angular furniture)
- casual (with a comfortable and natural/woody ambiance)
- country (accentuated with soft floral patterns)
- eclectic (featuring unique and artisanal or ethnic pieces)
- traditional (highlighting antique items and dark red wooden furniture)

By selecting one theme, you can significantly simplify choosing furniture that harmonizes with each other.

2. Next, consider your needs.

Consider the various necessities of you and your family and contemplate how furniture can enhance your everyday comfort. For instance, you and your spouse may require a spacious bed, such as a queen or king-size, while bedrooms for siblings could benefit from bunk beds or two single beds.

Do you have indoor pets? Consider that aspect as well. When selecting furniture for households with pets, it is essential to consider materials resistant to pet hair, stains, and scratches, such as leather or microfiber. In addition, opting for furniture with removable and washable covers can simplify maintenance and help keep your furniture clean and fresh.

3. Give importance to texture and textiles.

Carefully consider the composition of each furniture piece. Please note that certain fabrics and textures have a longer lifespan than others.

For instance, furniture crafted from nylon, olefin, and polyester is more durable than cotton, linen, and wool. Given the potentially high furniture cost, purchasing long-lasting pieces should be your primary objective. The choice of fabrics and textures serves as a valuable indicator of the expected longevity of your furniture.

4. Take into account the arrangement of each space.

Each room's size, lighting, interior design, and spatial configuration are essential. For instance, acquiring bulky furniture for a small room or a petite table for a spacious room would be impractical and would not look its best.

Have you ever seen a giant sofa in a small space? It's just not right. It is too much and dominates the room.

Furniture dimensions need to be proportionate to the size of the room. Believe it or not, there is scaled-down furniture for small spaces. There is such a thing as apartment furniture. Moreover, strive to ensure that the selected furniture pieces can harmoniously coexist without causing overcrowding.

Furniture adds vitality to our environments, improving the overall ambiance and achieving a cohesive aesthetic when chosen thoughtfully. Yet, the process of selecting suitable furniture extends beyond mere visual appeal. By implementing the above practical tips, you can transform your home into an inviting haven that welcomes and embraces all who enter.

The intricacies of turning your dream into a reality can be meticulous. However, the synergy of creativity and practicality emerged as a driving force, ensuring that aesthetics are harmoniously balanced with functionality. Through collaborative brainstorming and exploring innovative concepts, you can unearth the blueprint for a home that reflects your vision and caters to your needs. Hopefully, with the ideas shared, you can eagerly embrace the journey of transforming an abstract dream into a tangible and cherished living space.

Chapter Six: Keeping the Momentum Going: Creating Lasting Habits

"Energy is usually at its peak during the first part of your day, which means you should be completing habits that inspire or excite you about the day ahead." - S.J. Scott.

Healthy habits are crucial for sustaining a clean and organized home. Firstly, establishing a regular cleaning routine helps prevent dirt, dust, and clutter accumulation. You can maintain a clean-living environment by incorporating daily tidying, weekly deep cleaning, and regular decluttering sessions. These habits contribute to your home's aesthetics, promote better hygiene, and reduce the risk of allergies or respiratory issues. A clean home also provides calm and tranquility, making it a more enjoyable space to relax and unwind.

Furthermore, healthy habits play a vital role in organizing your home effectively. Habits such as assigning designated spaces for items, practicing the "one in, one out" rule, and regularly organizing and decluttering your belongings help create an organized living area. When everything has a proper place, it becomes easier to find what you need, saving you time and reducing stress.

Moreover, an organized home fosters a sense of order and promotes productivity. It allows you to focus on the task without being overwhelmed by distractions or searching for misplaced items.

Investing time and effort to create and maintain healthy habits for a clean and organized home improves physical health, mental well-being, and a more enjoyable living space.

Healthy Routine of Decluttering

Healthy habits thrive within the framework of a well-established routine. Integrating them into our daily or weekly practices creates a solid foundation for consistency and long-term commitment, making it easier to maintain and reap the benefits of a healthy lifestyle.

Here are some strategies on how to create a cleaning and decluttering routine:

1. Create attainable goals.

Attempting to declutter your entire home in a single day is an unfeasible endeavor that may result in overwhelming feelings. Instead, begin by setting small goals.

- Declutter and organize the kitchen pantry by the end of the week.
- Sort through and donate unused clothing items from the closet within the next two weeks.
- Clean and organize the home office desk and paperwork by the end of the month.
- Clear out and tidy up the garage by the end of the season.
- Create a designated space for children's toys and regularly declutter them every two weeks.

Occasionally, this process may feel like an ongoing cycle. For example, you tidy up one room only to find another in disarray. However, like with any task, achieving balance is crucial. So continuously adjust until you discover the optimal approach that works for you.

2. Begin small.

Take modest steps by allocating 10 to 15 minutes daily for decluttering. Then, as you establish a routine, gradually extend the duration of each session.

Building a habit entails constructing an environment that triggers automatic actions. It's not necessary to commence decluttering immediately; instead, focus on creating favorable circumstances for it to occur naturally.

3. Designate places for everything.

Establish an organized system where each item has its designated spot, adhering to the principle of "a place for everything and everything in its place." This practice minimizes clutter and simplifies the process of storing belongings.

Let's say your bedroom, what and where do you designate?

- Bedside essentials (e.g., books, glasses, phone) - the nightstand or bedside table
- Paperwork and documents - desk organizer on your workspace
- Jewelry and accessories - jewelry box, tray, or wall-mounted hooks near a vanity or dresser.
- Bed linens - a specific shelf or closet space
- Shoes - shoe rack or organizer near the entrance of the bedroom

4. Begin with spring cleaning.

When the state of your home feels excessively chaotic and overwhelming, it may be necessary to initiate a thorough deep cleaning. This process establishes a clean slate from which to commence. Once you have decluttered and organized everything, you can embrace a fresh start with a renewed system.

5. Be patient.

Decluttering and organizing are tasks you can do over time. This trait is crucial when building a routine for decluttering. Beautifying a space takes time and effort. Patience allows for a realistic understanding that progress will be gradual and requires consistent dedication.

In addition, building a routine requires establishing new habits and behaviors. It takes time for these habits to solidify and become ingrained in daily life. Patience enables persistence to stick to the routine even when motivation wanes.

Lastly, patience is essential when dealing with setbacks or obstacles during decluttering. It allows for a resilient mindset, enabling one to navigate challenges and stay committed to the routine despite setbacks.

In a society governed by rigid routines, attaining happiness and equilibrium can be a formidable quest. The initial stride toward achieving balance and contentment is how we organize and shape our daily routines.

Stay focused and dedicated to your decluttering routine, knowing that each small step brings you closer to a peaceful, organized living space that will enhance your well-being and productivity. Remember, consistency is critical. And if, in case, you stray, tell these to yourself:

I embrace the power of routines, knowing they provide structure and stability.

Daily, I prioritize my well-being by nurturing healthy habits that nourish my mind, body, and soul.

I am committed to establishing positive daily rituals that support my decluttering goals.

My routines are not limitations but catalysts for personal growth.

I am the architect of my habits; I shape a life of balance, productivity, and joy.

Chapter Seven: Dealing with Challenges: Overcoming Obstacles

"Until I had to move."

Can anyone else relate to this feeling? I spent many years working in property management, and over time, I accumulated more possessions than I could ever imagine. As a result, I had quite a collection.

It was exciting when I worked or lived on new buildings and got to score the furnishings from the last few units. However, the fun abruptly ended when I had to move.

It felt like a huge obstacle.

Moving to another house can be challenging due to the physical labor involved in packing and transporting belongings, the emotional attachment to familiar surroundings that may need to be left behind, and the logistical aspects of coordinating the move.

As I settled in, I panicked! There was so much to do with so little time!

I knew that what I was feeling was normal. What's not is that I am just letting the experience overwhelm me.

So, I looked at the bigger picture. I envisioned the outcome. And with that, I knew I could overcome any challenge with moving and decluttering.

Overcoming Obstacles

Decluttering or cleaning your home can be scary and overwhelming. But you will not be able to win it if you cower in fear.

When faced with difficulty in decluttering, it can be beneficial to determine the underlying reasons for your struggle. Frequently, once you have a clear understanding of the causes behind your battle, it becomes simpler to overcome it and eliminate the mess.

Here are some of those reasons and what you must do to eliminate them.

1. The "someday" attitude or keeping things for future use

People do this due to various psychological and practical reasons. Psychologically, individuals attach sentimental value to objects, associating them with memories, emotions, or aspirations. This sentimental attachment can make it difficult to let go of items, as people believe they might have future use or sentimental significance.

I know someone who had an extensive doll collection from American Girl to Barbie and the like. These dolls represent cherished memories of her childhood, evoking feelings of nostalgia. She believes she might pass them down to her children or display them in a nostalgic corner of their home, reinforcing her reluctance to let go.

From a practical standpoint, people may keep things for future use due to a sense of preparedness. They anticipate potential scenarios where the items might be helpful, even if those situations rarely materialize. This mindset stems from a desire to avoid regret or the fear of needing something later and not having it readily available.

How do you overcome this attitude on things you no longer need/use?

Overcoming your sentimental hold on things is a gradual process. But to start things off, you need to acknowledge the emotional attachment and recognize that memories are not tied solely to physical objects. Letting go of these items does not diminish the importance of their associated experiences.

2. "A waste of money" thinking

It is challenging to declutter with the thinking that throwing away or giving away stuff is a wasteful practice. For instance, you spent a fortune buying that ball gown you wore only once. Although you don't plan on wearing it again, it's hard to let go.

How do you divert your mind away from the money issue? - A change of mindset. Look at the benefits instead.

Giving rarely used stuff away is an opportunity to have a positive impact on whoever is on the receiving end. Donating old clothes, toys, and other items can benefit others in need, helping improve their quality of life.

Recognize the intrinsic value of generosity and the satisfaction of helping others, which can be more fulfilling than the temporary financial gain from holding onto unused possessions.

3. Lack of time

Decluttering requires time because it involves sorting each item and deciding what to keep, donate, or discard. Depending on the extent of clutter, it may involve going through multiple rooms or even an entire home, which can be time-consuming.

With other things on your plate, you may need more time (and energy) to tackle cleaning and decluttering. But you must make time. As Sam Levenson said, "Don't watch the clock; do what it does. Keep going."

To overcome the lack of time issue when decluttering, consider the following strategies:

A. Prioritize and set goals.

Start by identifying the areas or rooms that require the most attention and focus on those first. Then, set specific goals for each decluttering session to keep yourself motivated and on track.

B. Break it down into small tasks

Break it down into smaller, manageable tasks rather than attempting to tackle the entire decluttering process in one go. Allocate short bursts, such as 15-30 minutes, to declutter specific areas. A quick shot allows you to make progress even with limited time.

C. Create a schedule.

Set aside dedicated time slots on your calendar for decluttering sessions. Treat them as essential appointments and commit to sticking to them. Consistency is vital, even if it means dedicating a few minutes daily to decluttering.

D. Delegate and seek help.

Enlist the support of family members or friends to assist you in decluttering. Delegating tasks can help speed up the process and make it more enjoyable. Alternatively, consider hiring professional organizers who specialize in decluttering and organization.

Remember, accomplish decluttering through steps. By implementing these strategies and consistently dedicating small pockets of time to the process, you can gradually declutter your space and progress toward a more organized and serene environment.

4. Lacking a clear starting point

When decluttering, many people need help figuring out where to begin. Did you ever stare at a pile for a long time, wondering how to start?

Breathe deeply! Break it into manageable steps, solve it gradually, and simplify.

Complex or easy task first?

For some individuals, tackling the most challenging tasks first is their preferred approach. Initially, addressing the most difficult task makes the rest significantly easier.

Alternatively, starting with the most manageable tasks can be beneficial. It allows individuals to work their way up to more challenging tasks gradually. For example, accomplishing simple tasks like taking out the trash, doing laundry, or washing the dishes can provide a sense of achievement and enable them to proceed to more intensive tasks.

5. Lack of motivation

Motivation to declutter can be lacking for two significant reasons. Firstly, the overwhelming nature of the task can make it seem daunting and impossible, leading to a lack of motivation. Secondly, a lack of immediate consequences or visible rewards can diminish motivation, as the benefits of decluttering may take time to become apparent.

For the first challenge, it can be helpful to break them down into smaller, manageable steps. Then, prioritize and create a clear plan of action to tackle one task at a time. Finally, utilize time management techniques, such as setting specific deadlines or timers, to develop a sense of structure and progress.

Second, make up a list of possible consequences and rewards. Checking things off an extensive list is my favorite "attaboy" and "Yes, that is done!" for me.

Here's an example:

You are looking at your wardrobe cabinet. There's a sense of chaos inside your head as you gaze into the disorganized and overflowing clothes closet. The sight is overwhelming, with garments tangled together like a colorful, unruly tapestry.

The shelves once meant to hold neatly folded items, are now burdened under the weight of an excessive wardrobe. Clothes hang precariously from hangers, entangled and competing for space. A cascade of shirts, pants, and dresses spills onto the floor, forming fabric mounds obstructing the pathway. The disarray conjures feelings of frustration and a desperate longing for order.

If the mess itself is not enough motivation, here are the possible consequences if you leave it the way it is and the rewards you receive if you take action.

Consequences:

- Limited Space
- Increased stress every time you open your closet
- Poor clothing maintenance
- Unused clothing since you are unable to find them

Rewards:

- Aesthetic pleasure
- Enhanced personal style
- Improved clothing longevity
- More space

In the decluttering journey, it's essential to acknowledge and embrace the challenges that may arise. Decluttering is not just about organizing physical belongings; it can also be a transformative process that positively impacts your mindset and overall well-being.

Approach the task with patience, compassion, and a clear vision of the end goal—a space that reflects your values, enhances your daily life, and brings you joy. Decluttering is not a one-time event but an ongoing practice of conscious decision-making and intentional living.

Whatever the task, there will always be challenges. But like in any challenge, there will always be strategies to help you overcome the clutter and chaos.

Now, let's hear a woman's decluttering story.

I found myself in tears at a friend's house, finally admitting the state of my apartment. I compared it to the TV show 'Hoarders' to convey the severity of the situation, but they didn't fully believe me. Despite my outward appearance of being well-groomed and professionally dressed, internally, I was a mess of emotions.

My once lovely apartment had turned into a chaotic disaster zone, where I had to navigate to my bed carefully. I feel like having a seizure whenever I see items crammed in closets, overflowing drawers, cluttered kitchen cupboards and countertops, and piles of clothes, supplies, broken electronics, and other stuff. Even the furniture seemed suffocated by the mess.

I wanted to eliminate everything, leaving bare walls and empty spaces. But I couldn't bring myself to begin. Besides, where will I get the time to do this crazy project?

Thankfully, a more level-headed friend helped. She showed me what I could get if I took that necessary step. It was easy after.

I took a week off from work, and with her and my other friends' assistance, we systematically decluttered the apartment room by room.

We donated or recycled 25 boxes of various items and gave away bags of clothing, a couch, and an outdated computer. Everything that remained was assigned a designated place.

For example, clothes were hung neatly in the built-in closets, separating summer and winter attire. Everyday essentials were organized in transparent boxes or allocated drawers, while rarely used or specialized items were vacuum-sealed and adequately labeled.

She was right! The benefits were worth all this trouble.

The feeling of freedom that accompanied the decluttering process was remarkable. It allowed me to start anew and create a home I could be proud of.

For the first time in years, I had friends drop by for a cup of tea, a simple dinner, or drinks with snacks. Opening my home became a cause for celebration.

If she, as someone who felt broken and overwhelmed, managed to overcome her decluttering obstacles, you can too.

Chapter Eight: Creating Memories: Living Happily in Your Dream Home

Discovering happiness involves a combination of one's mindset and external circumstances rather than relying on a single secret. Making both minor and substantial adjustments can enhance one's level of happiness. Such adjustments include changes to your home.

Happiness could lie within your living environment. Your living space should serve as a sanctuary for relaxation and rejuvenation. Creating a joyful home contributes to a happier life, making it easier to appreciate moments of happiness and maintain a positive mindset. From decluttering to altering the lighting, there are straightforward methods to enhance your enjoyment within your home.

Happily Ever After

Our homes serve as more than just physical spaces. They are the backdrop for our lives, filled with cherished memories and experiences.

Creating a home that fosters enjoyment and meaningful experiences affects our emotional well-being profoundly. Our homes should be a sanctuary, a place where we can retreat from the outside world's demands and find solace.

When we invest time and effort into making our homes comfortable, welcoming, and reflective of our tastes, we cultivate a sense of belonging and security. This sense of emotional stability promotes relaxation, reduces stress, and enhances overall happiness.

Imagine coming home after a long, exhausting day at work. As you step into your carefully curated living room, adorned with your favorite colors and furniture, a feeling of comfort and familiarity washes over you.

The cozy ambiance, the soft lighting, and the personalized decor instantly put you at ease, melting away the day's stress and allowing you to unwind and recharge.

Our homes serve as a gathering place for our loved ones, providing an opportunity to strengthen and nurture our relationships. Creating an environment that promotes togetherness, warmth, and hospitality fosters more profound connections with family and friends. Don't you love looking at familiar faces with a backdrop of beauty and serenity?

Our homes reflect who we are and what we value. By enjoying our homes and creating memories within them, we contribute to building a legacy for ourselves and our families.

With Thanksgiving dinners, Sunday get-togethers, or simply having after-dinner drinks with friends and family, our homes become repositories of our personal history. These memories become a source of comfort and inspiration for future generations as they discover the stories, traditions, and values that shaped their family heritage.

Enjoying our homes and creating memories with loved ones is vital to a fulfilling and meaningful life. So, let us cherish and invest in our homes, for they can shape our memories, strengthen our bonds, and provide endless joy for ourselves and those we hold dear

I know; it's easier said than done. But with the help of the following, you can do it:

1. Use your home to spend time with your family.

Life has been incredibly hectic for everyone. We face constant change and a seemingly never-ending stream of challenges and responsibilities.

Time spent with family requires a conscious appreciation of the present moment. It involves immersing oneself in the joy and warmth of familial connections, embracing laughter, conversations, and shared experiences.

Your home serves as the ultimate sanctuary for bonding with family, offering a unique and irreplaceable space for connection. Within its walls, you and your family can be yourselves, free from external pressures and judgments. In addition, the familiarity and comfort of home foster an atmosphere of trust, enabling open and honest communication.

Shared experiences like meals, conversations, and laughter create lasting memories and strengthen relationships. In a nurturing home environment, family members can support, understand, and uplift one another, cultivating deep emotional bonds.

Whether through heartfelt conversations in the living room or playful moments in the backyard, the home provides the ideal backdrop for love, understanding, and cherished moments that shape lifelong connections.

Imagine this -

You sit around a crackling bonfire on a starry night in your newly landscaped backyard; the family swaps stories as you and your loved ones eat roasted marshmallows. Relish the warmth of each other's company. The laughter, the scent of the fire, and the genuine connections forged at that moment cultivate a true sense of contentment.

2. Have comfortable areas in your home.

Cozy and inviting areas promote relaxation and a sense of well-being. These spaces provide physical and emotional comfort, allowing individuals to unwind, recharge, and enjoy their surroundings.

It involves selecting comfortable furniture, incorporating soft textiles like pillows and blankets, using warm and soothing color schemes, and arranging the layout to encourage relaxation. Creating cozy spaces can enhance your (and your visitors') happiness and comfort, allowing you to escape daily stressors.

I love nothing better than coming home and plopping myself down on my plush sofa adorned with soft cushions and a warm, fuzzy blanket draped over the armrest. A gentle, dimmable lighting fixture casts a cozy glow across the room.

As I sink into the sofa, I reach for the remote control on a nearby side table, ready to indulge in my favorite TV shows or movies. The harmonious combination of comfort, ambiance, and entertainment in this carefully curated space provides a much-needed respite from the outside world's demands, allowing me to truly unwind and rejuvenate within the sanctuary of my own home.

3. Personalize.

The different areas in your home reflect your individuality and personal tastes. When you can remember your unique tastes and preferences in your living space, there is a sense of ownership, belonging, and identity. Surrounding yourself with items, colors, and decor that you genuinely love and resonate with will result in joy.

4. Go for functional organization.

Creating functional spaces catering to your needs and lifestyle makes your life easier. It could be a dedicated hobby corner, a home office reflecting your work style, or a cozy entertainment area that aligns with a preference for socializing.

Having these spaces ensures that the home is not just a place to live but a reflection of your interests.

Imagine having a dedicated hobby corner in your home where all your crafting supplies are neatly organized, with shelves and drawers to accommodate your materials. This functional space lets you quickly find and access everything you need, saving you time and frustration during your creative endeavors. Similarly, a thoughtfully designed home office tailored to your work style can enhance productivity and efficiency. From a comfortable ergonomic chair to a well-organized desk with designated compartments for stationery and documents, this functional workspace helps you stay focused and organized throughout your workday.

5. Go for aesthetics.

Aesthetics in a home can bring joy by creating visually pleasing and harmonious environments. When a home is aesthetically pleasing, it evokes positive emotions and a sense of delight.

Thoughtfully chosen colors, textures, patterns, and visual elements can create a sense of balance, harmony, and beauty, which can profoundly impact your mood and overall well-being. Aesthetically pleasing homes will have a sense of tranquility, provide inspiration and creativity, and uplift the spirits of the residents and visitors.

Imagine walking into a living room adorned with a palette of soft pastel colors complemented by natural materials like wood and stone.

The space features carefully curated artwork and decor items that align with a specific theme, like coastal or bohemian. The furniture promotes a sense of openness and flow. Soft, ambient lighting fixtures create a warm and inviting atmosphere.

Olivia had always felt a deep connection to her family home. It held a treasure trove of memories, from childhood laughter to family gatherings. However, as the years went by, the house became cluttered and chaotic and no longer reflected the warmth and love it once exuded.

Determined to restore the magic, Olivia embarked on a journey to redesign and declutter their family home.

With unwavering determination, Olivia began by sorting through every nook and cranny, meticulously deciding which items were truly cherished and had lost meaning. Then, one by one, she let go of the unnecessary clutter, freeing up space and breathing new life into the rooms. As she continued, Olivia tapped into her creative side, envisioning a fresh and inviting aesthetic that would bring happiness to all who entered.

Olivia's design efforts created evoked joy and comfort. She chose soothing colors and incorporated natural elements, infusing each room with serenity. In addition, she meticulously selected furniture, artwork, and decor that reflected her family's personality, creating a space that felt uniquely theirs.

As the transformation unfolded, Olivia's family noticed the changes and embraced their home's newfound order and beauty.

The decluttered spaces allowed for more effortless movement and encouraged deeper connections. The living room became a cozy haven for family movie nights, with laughter filling the air. The kitchen is a hub where delicious meals are prepared and shared with love. Finally, the bedroom became a sanctuary for rest and rejuvenation, inviting peaceful dreams and well-deserved relaxation.

The impact of Olivia's efforts extended beyond the physical transformation of the house. The renewed home created an environment that fostered lasting memories and strengthened family bonds. Every corner held a story, every room radiated warmth, and every shared moment became a cherished experience.

Through her determination and love for her family, Olivia's redesign and decluttering efforts transformed their physical space and revitalized their lives. Once weighed down by disarray and chaos, the family members now exude joy and contentment. Their interactions have become more harmonious and loving as they no longer feel overwhelmed by their surroundings.

Olivia, her husband, and their kids spend more time together, engaging in activities that nourish their bonds, such as family game nights and shared meals. As a result, the children's grades have improved significantly, reflecting their increased focus and motivation in a peaceful environment. In addition, Olivia and her husband have rekindled their romance, finding solace in a serene and inviting bedroom.

The family's revitalized lives are evident in their radiant smiles, relaxed demeanor, and vibrant atmosphere that now fills their home. Their home became a testament to the power of a nurturing environment, where love, happiness, and meaningful memories flourished for years.

Conclusion

An essential part of your journey toward a beautiful home is acknowledging the power of your actions. It would help if you believed that your efforts have the potential to make a significant difference. After all, this is the dream home we are talking about.

As you declutter and organize, remind yourself that simplicity is liberating. Let go of possessions that no longer serve you and create space for what truly matters. Each item you discard is a step towards a more purposeful and meaningful existence. Embrace the lightness and clarity that comes with each bag donated, each shelf organized, and each room transformed.

It's natural to face challenges and moments of doubt during the process. But remember, progress is not always linear. Give yourself permission to make mistakes and learn from them. Celebrate the small victories along the way. Recognize the effort you're putting in and its positive impact on your life.

Visualize the result—the home you've always dreamed of. Envision the peaceful sanctuary, the vibrant gathering spaces, and the cozy nooks.

Let this vision inspire you to push forward, even when faced with obstacles. Believe that you can create a home that nurtures your spirit and brings you joy daily.

As you make progress, find joy in the journey. Embrace the process of discovery and exploration. Let your creativity flourish as you choose lively colors, lush fabrics, and beautiful decor that resonate with your soul. Revel in the delight of arranging and rearranging, finding the perfect spot for each particular item. Finally, embrace the opportunity to express your unique personality and taste through your home's design.

In moments of weariness, remind yourself of a beautiful and organized home's positive impact on your overall well-being. A tidy environment promotes a clear mind, reduces stress, and fosters productivity.

So, let these final affirmations guide you along your journey:

I deserve a beautiful and organized home that brings me joy.

Every step I take brings me closer to the home of my dreams.

I embrace simplicity and find liberation in decluttering.

Each effort I make transforms my home and enhances my well-being.

I can create a space that reflects my unique personality and taste.

My home is a canvas for my aspirations and a catalyst for my personal growth.

I find joy in the journey of creating my dream home.

Keep these affirmations close to your heart as you continue your journey. Let them continuously inspire you as you create the home of your imagination.

You can create a space that reflects your personality and style and supports and enhances your daily life. Your dream home is within your grasp. So, embrace the journey, stay motivated, and never lose sight of the incredible transformation you bring to your home and life.

So, take that first step today. Then, start creating a beautiful, organized, and happy home.

References:

https://abundantlifewithless.com/uncluttered/

https://www.veranda.com/home-decorators/g32031382/decluttering-cleaning-quotes/

https://www.smart-storage.co.uk/2019/06/the-benefits-of-a-decluttered-home/

https://www.smart-storage.co.uk/2019/06/the-benefits-of-a-decluttered-home/

https://www.cdc.gov/nchs/products/databriefs/db460.htm#:~:text=Key%20findings-,Data%20from%20the%20National%20Health%20Interview%20Survey,and%20non%2DHispanic%20Asian%20adults.

https://www.forbes.com/sites/joshuabecker/2019/04/05/how-decluttering-her-home-changed-this-young-mothers-entire-life/

https://www.buzzsprout.com/1502644/7178560-denzel-washington-dreams-without-goals-are-just-dreams-and-they-ultimately-fuel-disappointment

https://www.successconsciousness.com/blog/goal-setting/importance-of-setting-goals/

https://simplelionheartlife.com/before-you-start-decluttering/

https://www.becomingminimalist.com/letting-go/

https://www.hellaproperty.com/blog/home-organizing/declutter-your-home/

https://www.inc.com/peter-economy/17-marie-kondo-quotes-that-will-help-you-organize-get-control-of-your-life-work.html

https://popularvedicscience.com/ayurveda/general-health/ways-clutter-impacts-productivity/

https://simpleeverydayhome.com/how-to-clean-the-messiest-room-in-your-house/

https://scrubnbubbles.com/house-cleaning-tips/a-step-by-step-guide-to-deep-cleaning-a-bedroom/

https://www.healthline.com/health/healthy-home-guide#how-to-clean-a-kitchen

https://www.thespruce.com/how-to-mop-a-floor-1901114

https://www.lung.org/clean-air/at-home/indoor-air-pollutants/cleaning-supplies-household-chem

https://www.architectureartdesigns.com/tips-for-choosing-the-right-furniture-for-your-house/

https://www.clubfurniture.com/blogs/news/how-to-choose-the-right-furniture-for-your-home

https://www.getorganizedwizard.com/blog/2022/06/how-to-be-consistent-and-make-decluttering-a-routine/

https://www.getorganizedwizard.com/blog/2019/07/my-house-is-so-cluttered-i-dont-know-where-to-start/

https://simplelionheartlife.com/struggle-to-declutter/

15 Bonus Home Decorating "Must Dos"
To Have The Home You Imagine

- Lighting is the biggest deal in a room, dark rooms are never good except to sleep in.
- Use 2 to 3 different kinds of lighting, torchers, lamps, ceiling lights, and natural light. Depending on the room orientation you may need different lighting.
- Hang Pictures at Eye Level.
- Triangles and circles should be your guide for balance when hanging pictures.
- Cluster things (table accessories) that look alike, in color, size, theme, and era, apply the 3 to 5 item rule here too.
- Cluster Pictures and accessories in numbers 3 or 5 (odd numbers make things interesting).
- Place furniture facing other furniture away from the wall. Furniture is for people sitting and talking. Group it together.
- Don't Push coaches and chairs against the wall EVER!
- Having 3 Colors as a theme throughout the house adds depth and interest.
- Add 3 textures in rooms: leather, wool, silk, fiber, pillows, and throws.
- Fireplaces should be in the center of the room. (sometimes not possible).
- Don't Put your TV in your living space if possible. Hide it if possible.
- Reminder, too much is never enough.
- A clean look makes a room look larger.
- Don't Cover your windows too much. Using see-through window coverings creates privacy but allows light to enter.

Congrats!   Note from the Anita Marie:

You've reached the end of the book!

Thank you for finishing The Home You Imagine!

Looks like you enjoyed it!

If so, would you mind taking 30 seconds and Pop Onto Amazon and leave a quick review? Thank you ahead of time!!

We worked hard to bring you an enjoyable book! Plus, it helps authors like us to produce more books like this in the future!

Made in the USA
Middletown, DE
06 October 2023

40373428R00044